I Can

Doing the Right Thing

Show I Care

Written by Jenette Donovan Guntly
Photographed by Michael Jarrett

GARETH STEVENS
GS
PUBLISHING
A World Almanac Education Group Company

Please visit our web site at: www.garethstevens.com
For a free color catalog describing Gareth Stevens Publishing's list of high-quality books
and multimedia programs, call 1-800-542-2595 (USA) or 1-800-387-3178 (Canada).
Gareth Stevens Publishing's fax: (414) 332-3567.

Library of Congress Cataloging-in-Publication Data

Guntly, Jenette Donovan.
   (Show you understand)
   I can show I care / written by Jenette Donovan Guntly; photographed by Michael Jarrett.
      p. cm. — (Doing the right thing)
   ISBN 0-8368-4247-2 (lib. bdg.)
   1. Caring—Juvenile literature.   I. Jarrett, Michael, 1956- .   II. Title.
   BJ1475.G86   2004
   177'.7—dc22
                                                          2004045297

This North American edition first published in 2005 by
Gareth Stevens Publishing
A World Almanac Education Group Company
330 West Olive Street, Suite 100
Milwaukee, WI 53212 USA

This edition copyright © 2005 by Gareth Stevens, Inc. Original edition copyright © 2002 by Creative Teaching Press, Inc.,
P.O. Box 2723, Huntington Beach, CA 92647-0723. First published in the United States in 2002 as *Show You Understand:
Learning about Compassion and Caring* by Creative Teaching Press, Inc. Original text copyright © 2002 by Regina G. Burch.

A special thanks to Erin Kominsky and the wonderful staff at Weaver Elementary School in Los Alamitos, CA.

Photographer: Michael Jarrett
Gareth Stevens designer: Kami M. Koenig

Printed in the United States of America

1 2 3 4 5 6 7 8 9 08 07 06 05 04

I can show I care!

My brother wants to learn to read.

I show him what I know.

Being new at school is hard.

We smile and say hello.

Matthew drops his pile of books.

We lend a helping hand.

Vicki feels very sad.

I show I understand.

Samantha sits alone at lunch.

I keep her company.

When no one knows what game to play,

just leave it up to me!

We take turns. It's only fair.
Playing together shows we care.